Merry Christmas
Barbara

♡ Katie

Barbra Streisand

Barbra Streisand

Nick Yapp

FALL RIVER PRESS

contents

chapter 1

the early years

Barbra Streisand's indomitable spirit was forged in her childhood. She hardly knew her father, her mother gave her little support, and her stepfather told her she was ugly. But she always knew exactly what she wanted to do – to sing – and in the early 1960s she made her professional debut. Her mother was unimpressed, telling Barbra: "Your voice is very thin. You need eggs in your milk to make your voice stronger…" There were two theatrical false starts in her beloved New York: *The Insect Comedy* (three performances) and *Another Evening with Larry Stoones* (one performance) and then came success

i can get it for you wholesale

Barbara Joan Streisand was born on April 24, 1942 in Williamsburg, Brooklyn. Her parents were New Yorkers by birth; her grandparents were immigrants who had fled Nazi persecution in Vienna. Barbara (the second "a" was dropped later) barely knew her father, who died when she was fifteen months old, and had an uncomfortable relationship with the step-father who came on the scene some five years later.

Streisand started singing in earnest while at Erasmus Hall High School, but her mother counselled against show business, recommending that Streisand learn to type and follow in her footsteps as a school secretary. It was a waste of time. The young Streisand was determined to make anyone and everyone in showbiz listen to her.

She made her club debut at *The Lion* in Greenwich Village and brought the house down. The next venue was *Bon Soir* on Eighth Avenue. Here, one critic suggested that Streisand "be filed and forgotten". She responded: "That old fart! What does he know?" She went on singing and headed for Broadway.

Elbowing all competition aside, Streisand grabbed the role of Yetta Tessye Marmelstein in *I Can Get It For You Wholesale*, practically rewriting the character to fit her own age and personality. Once the show opened, Streisand stopped it nightly with her four-minute solo.

Left: The twenty-one-year old Streisand singing at a Fight for Sight benefit concert in 1963.
Right: The original cover of Streisand's award-winning first album, released in 1963. The herringbone vest and blouse with the Peter Pan collar were a foretaste of Streisand's future world of fashion.

the first album

Streisand's career took off like a rocket. From the very start, the voice was glorious, and precociously mature in its range and control. Streisand could deliver everything from the wistful fragility of a ballad to the brazen power of a showbiz belter. She could communicate joy, sadness, love, longing, fun, fulfilment, and chutzpah. On top of this, she was a great judge of musical material, whether it was hot off the press or from the back catalogue.

Songwriters loved her. Harold Arlen, composer of *Somewhere Over the Rainbow* and thirty-seven years Streisand's senior,

wrote the sleeve note for her debut LP, *The Barbra Streisand Album*. In a paean of praise he advised buyers of the album to "Watch, listen and remember: I told you so". Julie Styne marvelled at her talent, but admitted that Streisand had "a tendency to show off a bit. She was always shoving shovelsful of talent in your face..."

In 1963 *The Barbra Streisand Album* reached the top of the charts and won two Grammy Awards, for Album of the Year and for Best Female Vocal Performance. In the same year she released *The Second Barbra Streisand Album*, which reached

Number Two in the charts. It was an auspicious start, a dream start for anyone else, but Streisand had her sights set higher. Recording studios were fine, but superstars had to do more than just sing.

Left: John F. Kennedy, President of the United States, signs his autograph for Streisand, May 24, 1963. The occasion was the Washington Press Correspondents' Dinner.

Right: Kennedy and Streisand in conversation at the Dinner. All her life she has been a fan of Kennedy's politics, regarding him as a man who found "reasonable solutions" to complicated problems in "turbulent times".

The Broadway musical *Funny Girl* opened at the Winter Gardens Theater on March 26, 1964. For the next twenty-one months, Streisand sang twelve numbers a show eight times a week, in the role of Jewish singer and comedienne Fanny Brice. She received rave reviews from the critics. Her picture was on the cover of *Life* magazine. The original cast album, which featured two of the biggest musical guns in Streisand's armoury (*Don't Rain on My Parade* and *People*) went to Number Two in the charts.

The career was doing fine, and Streisand was meeting exciting people, among them the President of the United States. In May 1963, wearing a gown that she had designed, she met John Kennedy at the Washington Press Correspondents' Dinner. Streisand never made any secret of her politics. She was not just a Democrat, she was "a feminist, Jewish, opinionated, liberal woman". In a typical breach of accepted etiquette, she asked JFK for his autograph, claiming it was for her mother.

Left: Streisand as "Bessie May" performs the hillbilly number on the CBS *Bob Hope Comedy Special*, June 9, 1963 *(from left to right)* Dean Martin, Streisand, Bob Hope.
Right: Streisand duets with her idol on the *Judy Garland Show* in 1965.

onwards and upwards

By the summer of 1963, Streisand had made only one album (*The Barbra Streisand Album*, released on February 25, 1963) and appeared in one Broadway show (*I Can Get It For You Wholesale*). Such was her impact on the entertainment world, however, that she was already being invited to perform alongside top stars on primetime television shows. On June 9, 1963, she made a guest appearance with Dean Martin on *The Bob Hope Comedy Special*.

She sang two solo numbers on the show: *Any Place I Hang My Hat Is Home,* written by two of her ardent admirers, Johnny Mercer and Harold Arlen; and Peter Matz's yearning *Gotta Move.* Matz was to Streisand as Nelson Riddle was to Sinatra, a musical director and arranger with complete understanding of how best to serve the voice he was accompanying. He was to play a key role throughout Streisand's career.

The high-spot of *The Bob Hope Comedy Special* was a hillbilly sketch performed by Hope, Martin, and Streisand. They sang *Jimmy Crack Corn* (with new lyrics that included a swipe at Secretary of State Dean Rusk) and fooled around. As "Bessie May" Streisand showed impeccable comic timing and appeared outrageously confident in such august company. In reality she was plagued by her customary stage-fright in front of a studio audience.

By the mid 1960s, Barbra Streisand was already an American icon, with a support base that included a wide variety of sub-sections of society. In the words of Isobel Lennart, who wrote the screenplay for *Funny Girl,* she had already "made life better for a helluva lot of homely girls" – "homely" being shorthand for "not classically beautiful". She had followed in the footsteps of Judy Garland as a heroine of the gay community. Dissidents and would-be rebels loved her outspokenness. The showbiz establishment relished her box-office appeal. And music lovers adored every note she sang. It was a coalition that was to serve her faithfully for the whole of her career.

In April 1964, immediately after the Broadway opening of *Funny Girl,* Streisand's portrait appeared on the cover of *Time.* The editors commissioned a painting. It turned out to be one that didn't do her justice. "

Left: (*clockwise from top*) At the Bergdorf Goodman studios in New York City, Barbra Streisand watches a TV playback on herself during the taping of the TV special *My Name is Barbra*; Streisand tries on a costume for the special; sitting on a kettledrum during rehearsals; presenting her less favourite profile.

Right: A still from the childhood sequence on *My Name is Barbra*, recorded on April 11, 1965.

my name is barbra

Streisand was not quite twenty-three years old when she made her own first television special. As in the case of her first two albums, she made sure that her name was in the title, a shrewd but by then almost unnecessary publicity ploy. Critics raved. The United Press International spoke for many when it called the show "a pinnacle in American show business, in any form, in any period. She is so great it is shocking, something like being in love... She may well be the most supremely talented and complete popular entertainer that this country has ever produced... She touches you to your toes. And then she knocks you out." The show won five Emmys, including Outstanding Individual Achievement, and the Peabody Award for Outstanding Program Achievement. The album of the same name, released two weeks later, won Streisand her third Grammy for Best Female Vocal Performance.

Fake and Genuine Streisand. **Above:** Debbie Reynolds struts her version of Streisand in 1965.

Right: The real Streisand poses with her Emmy at the Emmy Awards ceremony in the Grand Ballroom of the Hilton Hotel, New York, September 12, 1965. The Award was for Outstanding Achievements in Entertainment.

the unflattering copy, the totally glamorous original

At school, Streisand had been nicknamed "Big Beak". Still today, people argue as to what part her looks played in her early success – did she succeed because of, or in spite of, her face. Late in her career, Streisand said of her looks: "Some things improve with age", but very few commentators have shared her stepfather's view that she was ugly. Her face was different. One of her biographers, Tom Santopietro, reckoned that it was not the nose but the eyes that jarred. They were too small and too close together. They were saved, however, by the intensity of their blueness.

When it came to fashion, from the word "go", Streisand's dress sense was eclectic and adventurous. She was never scared to wear an outfit that might be labelled "outrageous". However flamboyant the dress, she had the personality to make sure it was only an accessory.

Right: Barbra Streisand in her dressing room at the Winter Gardens Theater in New York during the run of *Funny Girl*, October 6, 1965.

behind the scenes

Streisand's triumphant entry into popular music was a break with tradition. The very early 1960s was still the age of Rosemary Clooney, Dinah Shore, Jo Stafford and Doris Day – pretty, wholesome, well-groomed chanteuses who sang wistful love songs and cute up-tempo numbers. Streisand had a different portfolio.

Streisand has always been a perfectionist – an artist who gives her best and expects the best from others. Like all great artists, she has taken an intense interest in the material with which she has worked. Rumor has it that, early in her career, this was to see if there was some way she could enlarge her part in proceedings. She is also someone who fiercely rejects anything that reeks of insincerity.

The composer Julie Styne wrote of her: "There is only one way to deal with Barbra Streisand, tell her the truth. If you don't tell her the truth then you're going to have problems." But when it comes to criticism, even Streisand has always been highly vulnerable. Her private life is private. She resents any invasion of that privacy, even if it's merely a helicopter flying too low over her Malibu home.

color me barbra

Two weeks after finishing her Broadway run in *Funny Girl,* Streisand began work on her second TV special, *Color Me Barbra.* She was backed by a tried and tested team. The executive producer was Martin Ehrlichman, who had been her personal manager since the very early days, and once again her musical director was Peter Matz. But Streisand anguished over the whole project, which was wildly ambitious in its staging.

The first act included a sequence filmed at the Philadelphia Museum of Art in which Streisand appeared as a maid, Marie Antoinette, a Modigliani-inspired Frenchwoman, and Nefertiti. Things went wrong. "As soon as the music taping began," she later explained, "two of our new Marconi cameras gave out. There were no replacements. That left us with only one camera for the whole opening selection."

Left and above: Streisand in the
Philadelphia Museum of Art, dressed as
Nefertiti for the opening sequence of *Color
Me Barbra*, January 23, 1966. The New York
Metropolitan Museum had turned down
the request to film there.

Left and right: Two stills from *Color Me Barbra* – Streisand on the trampoline; a shot from the animal sequence in which she performed with a tiger and a leopard. There was consternation in the studio when one of the big cats broke out of the cage. The beast met its match in Streisand.

Above: Streisand in front of the TV cameras during the three-ring circus segment of *Color Me Barbra*. *The New York Times* reported: "the horses reared, the penguins got sick... the leopard refused to pose..."

Right: Streisand enjoys a playback of a part of the show. "Give me Julie Andrews any day," said one of the electricians.

As soon as she had finished work on the TV special *Color Me Barbra*, Streisand set off for London and a three month West End run in *Funny Girl*. Legend has it that she discovered that she was pregnant on the show's opening night, but by then Streisand was already considerably larger than life, and legend was untrustworthy. It is true, however, that some of the show's choreography – including the famous leap on to the *chaise longue* – had to be altered because of her condition, and that, while in London and recovering from a cold, she recorded one of her most popular albums, *A Christmas Album*.

Two pictures taken at the press launch of the London West End production of *Funny Girl*, March 20, 1966. Streisand was about to find out that she was pregnant. Both photographs were taken by Terry Fincher of the London *Daily Express*.

my name is iconoclasm

While rehearsing for *Funny Girl*'s London run, Streisand took time off to visit Paris and to go shopping for clothes that she would wear in her next TV special. She paid six visits to Dior's fashion house, arriving late on four of them. Dior delayed the start for her convenience, but in so doing, annoyed the Duchess of Windsor, who was also present. Streisand noted that the Duchess looked "grouchy".

If she was in any way overawed by Paris fashion, Streisand made sure no-one noticed. On February 2, 1966 she arrived

at a fashion show in a jaguar suit and hat that she had designed herself. A fellow visitor, Marlene Dietrich (*above, far right*) appeared bemused. The *Vogue* photographer who was present made sure he photographed her, and Streisand herself made sure it made the cover of *Vogue*.

As one of the world's Ten Best-Dressed Women, she was critical of Paris prices but admired the quality of the work: 'They sew buttons better here...' There are varying legends as to just how good a customer she was. One story says she bought day

dresses, suits, evening gowns, sports clothes, hats, shoes, and coats. Another says she bought nine outfits. Estimates as to how much she spent range from $20,000 to $150,000.

Above, right, and overleaf: Streisand
plays up to the camera for a photo shoot
in New York's Central Park.

The young Streisand allowed herself little time out to look back on her phenomenal personal achievements. In just a few years she had progressed from early off-Broadway flops to award-winning success on stage, screen, film, and television. Professionally, she had gone further and faster than Judy Garland, an artist whom she admired and with whom she had much in common in terms of unhappiness and vulnerability.

After such a whirlwind ride, many performers might have suffered from attacks of self-doubt, might have asked themselves "where do I go from here?" Early showbiz success on such a massive scale has its down-side. Success has to breed success. She had to live up to the praise that had been showered on her. "She is mad with talent," wrote Maurice Chevalier, "and more gifted than any human being should be permitted to be."

Richard Rodgers commented: "No one is talented enough to sing with the depth of a fine cello or the lift of a climbing bird. Nobody that is, except Barbra..." But the human voice is a fickle instrument, capable of deserting its owner, and Streisand had already been liberally generous in the use of hers. Critics and fans alike were beginning to wonder how much longer both star and vocal chords could keep the magic coming.

Left and opposite: Streisand waves the Skull and Crossbones flag in Central Park, New York.

Three studies by photographer Bill Eppridge of Streisand at the recording sessions of the *Color Me Barbra* album, March 30, 1966.
Far right: Streisand's concern at a play back is watched (*at rear left, in glasses*) by Michel Legrand, who shared the musical arrangements for the album with Don Costa and Peter Matz.

look and *life*

Both *Look* and *Life* magazines published in-depth articles on Streisand to mark the transmission of her TV special *Color Me Barbra* and the release of the album featuring songs from the show. Diana Lurie, writing in *Life*, called Streisand "the undisputed queen of musical comedy, television and records..." But Lurie also noted the edginess and insecurity that permeated much of Streisand's work. "Everybody knows Streisand is on top. So does she. And the more she is hailed, the more scared and insecure she feels."

Streisand herself admitted it. "I win awards and everything but one of these days something is going to bomb. It's a scary thing. It can all suddenly fall apart." The moment she completed a take for a section of the *Color Me Barbra* show, Streisand ran to the control room to watch and hear the play back. She then turned to the director, Dwight Hemion, and said: "I am waiting for you to say whether I am great or lousy. You said nothing. I must know what you think or I am depressed."

In *Look* magazine, Thomas B. Morgan reported that Streisand worked for almost thirty-two hours on the special without a real break. "She slaved, she fuelled. Hour by hour, she ate pretzels, potato chips, peppermint sour balls, a hero sandwich, pickles, a corned-beef sandwich, coffee ice cream, roast beef on rye, Swiss cheese on white, hamburger, Danish pastry, *petit fours*..." The list went on and on. But she complained only once – that her feet hurt – and happily her husband Elliott Gould was there to apply massage.

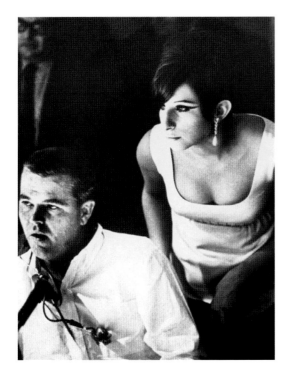

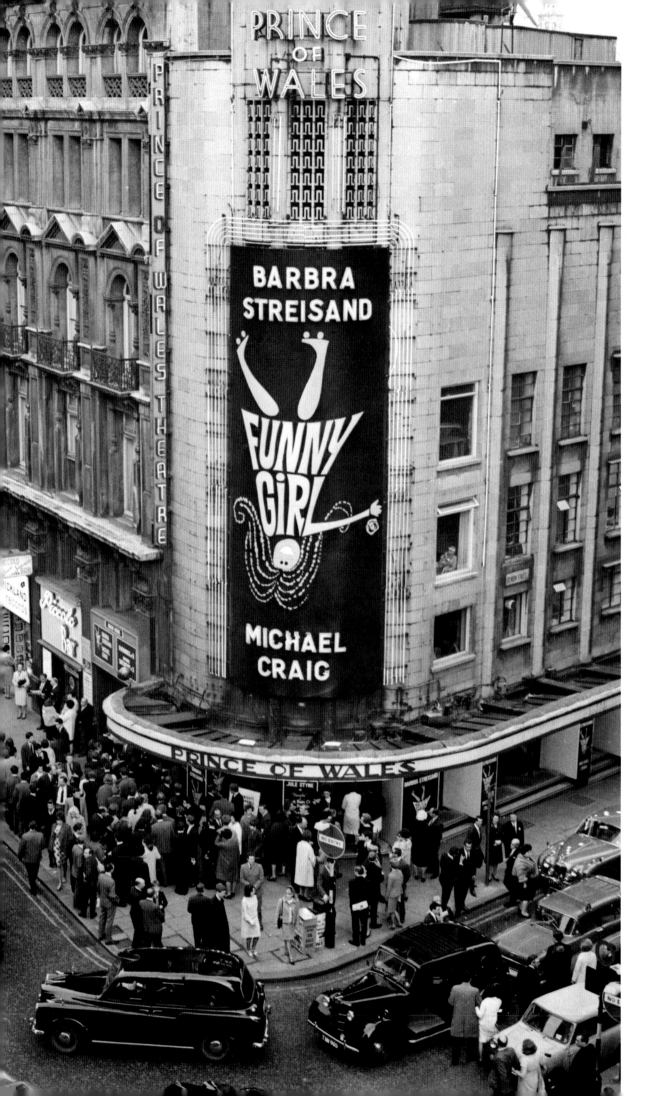

Left and above: Crowds form to see *Funny Girl* at the Prince of Wales Theatre in London's West End, April 29, 1966. It was the night when Streisand was indisposed and her place was taken by Lisa Shane.

Two portraits of Barbra Streisand by the photographer Bill Eppridge.
Left: The famous nose, taken from Streisand's preferred side – her left side.
Right: Streisand poses with Sadie, one of the many pet dogs she has had in her life.

the nose

In a 1977 *Playboy* interview, Streisand attributed the unique sound of her voice to her nose. "It's my deviated septum," she said. "If ever I had my nose fixed it would ruin my career." And in the beginning, when she was a night club singer (where the lights were low), or a recording artist (where the product is purely audio), or a musical comedy star (with a considerable distance between performer and audience), the nose was not a problem. When she entered the world of television and movies, however, the nose could have become an issue.

It was undeniably long and it was hawkish. While Streisand had deliberately grown long fingernails to thwart her mother's ambition that her daughter become a typist, there was little she could do about the nose, other than prefer to have it photographed from the left side. In the animal section of the *Color Me Barbra* special, Streisand bravely and musically compared her profile to that of an anteater for the song *We Have So Much In Common*.

The ultimate solution to the problem of living with the nose was, however, simple. Streisand decided to present herself, in the way she dressed and behaved, as the most glamorous woman around. It was not simply a matter of posh frocks. There were all the fashion accessories to be considered – bags, gloves, hats, and jewellery – and a white French poodle named Sadie, who not only featured in the TV special, but also had her own VIP chair on the set of *Funny Girl*.

Below: Streisand in full flow and full stride along the 200 foot walkway into the audience during the second half of the *Happening in Central Park* concert.

Left: A section of the audience in the Sheep Meadow area of Central Park. Six television cameras and a film camera mounted on a helicopter captured the concert from almost every conceivable angle.

the happening in central park

In June 1967, Streisand took a weekend off from filming *Funny Girl* in Hollywood and flew to New York to give a single concert. It was called *A Happening in Central Park,* it was free, and it attracted an audience of 135,000 adoring fans. It was also an exhausting process for Streisand, who spent Friday night rehearsing until late, working out the camera blocking, trying on a range of gowns and exploring different hairstyles with her hairdresser, Fred Glaser.

On Saturday, it rained on her parade. "I mean it absolutely poured," said Phil Ramone, sound engineer on the album of the concert. "So we never had a check with her or her band. The orchestra said, "We can't come out here with our violins and beautiful oboes, it's just too damp." They had a point. The humidity led to some slightly off-key playing in Levin and Shafer's *He Touched Me.* Around six, however, the weather cleared and the orchestra relented. The concert went ahead.

Security was tight. Streisand had received death threats following the conclusion of the Six Day War. In Streisand's own words: "I was afraid that somebody might take a shot at me during the concert. So I started walking around the stage fast. And I forgot my words (to *Value*), which is an actor's nightmare. And that frightened me – that absolute lack of control." Such was her concern at what happened, she waited another twenty-seven years before giving another live concert.

Left and above: Two moments and two contrasting Streisand moods from the *Happening in Central Park Concert.* Apart from the death threat and the momentary loss of words, Streisand's ever-present stage fright was activated when the audience suddenly surged toward the stage. Her subsequent withdrawal from live performances almost certainly lost her record sales, though she was still the best-selling female vocalist in the world.

The Diva Descends. An elegantly clad
Streisand enjoys a night out at the Garnier
Opera, Paris, 1968.

barbra in paris

In 1966, while in Paris, Streisand spoke of her hopes and fears in an interview she gave to Polly Devlin for *Vogue* magazine. "At eighteen I dreamed of success and it was much easier because dreams are clear. When you reach success it's no longer exciting. You have to learn... that it's never as good as the dream. It's sort of anti-climactic... I don't think I'll ever have enough confidence. I'm never satisfied with anything I do..."

"...I never think it good enough. Sometimes when I listen to a record I don't get bothered but I don't get ecstatic either – I hate it when I hear the mistakes. When photographers, people in the street, rush after me, I always think they are going to hit me or something, people coming after me...." When she gave the interview, she was not well, and said that she was depressed, but added that she meant what she had said about success.

Some of Streisand's problems arose because she was so talented. She was too good at too many things. In a way, her whole persona was too much of everything. She has been labelled too Brooklyn, too Jewish, too eccentric, too oddball, too old-fashioned in her choice of songs, too gay in her style, too obscure, too fussy, and a control freak. The criticisms, and the pain, came with the job. There was bound to be a fall from grace somewhere over the rainbow.

In less elaborate costume and with ladylike handbag, Streisand spends time out to deal with paperwork, while the *paparazzi* hover in the background.

funny girl on screen

Forty years on, those who remember the moment when the Best Actress Award was presented at the 1969 Academy Award ceremony do so for two reasons: it was the first tie in the history of the Academy, and one of the two recipients wore a pantsuit that left little to the imagination. The recipients were Katharine Hepburn, for her portrayal of Eleanor of Aquitaine in James Goodman's *A Lion in Winter*, and Streisand for her screen recreation of Fanny Brice in *Funny Girl*. Hepburn was not the wearer of the pantsuit.

The film was a huge commercial success. *Funny Girl* grossed over $57 million at the box office, making it the biggest taker of the year, ahead of *2001 – A Space Odyssey*, *The Odd Couple* and *Bullitt*. William Wyler brought experience and professionalism to its direction, and the musical numbers were wonderfully staged by Herb Ross. But it was Streisand who made the film sell then, and decades later, it's Streisand who makes the film sell now.

She was twenty-six years old when she made the film, and she still felt that she had a great deal to prove to the world. Consequently, she threw every last joule of energy that she possessed into bringing Fanny to life – in joy and misery, in good times and bad times, in sickness and in health. It is an exhausting performance to watch, with Streisand propelling herself into movie stardom. The wonder is that she had anything left for the next forty years of her career.

Left: Streisand at the Academy Award ceremony in Santa Monica, April 10, 1968.
Right: Sammy Davis Junior receives his Oscar on behalf of Leslie Bricusse and Anthony Newley. Streisand was introduced by Bob Hope. It is said that Ray Stark, the producer of *Funny Girl*, was furious at how Streisand looked on television. He took exception to both Streisand's dress and hairstyle, believing that they would be bad publicity for the upcoming movie.

the lure of hollywood

At the 40th Academy Awards ceremony in 1968, held at the Santa Monica Civic Auditorium in California, Streisand presented the Best Song Award to Sammy Davis Junior. The song – *Talk With the Animals* – had nothing to do with either of them. It was written by Leslie Bricusse and Anthony Newley, and sung (or, rather, chanted) by Rex Harrison in the movie *Dr. Doolittle*. Streisand would have to wait another year for her own Oscar.

But Streisand had now achieved what had always been her ultimate goal – to become firmly established in Tinseltown. She once described herself as being "simple, complex, generous, selfish, unattractive, beautiful, lazy and driven" – four paradoxical pairs that seemingly cancel each other out. But, though it's possible to be a mixture of generous and selfish (everyone has his or her off days), the "driven" quality always overcame what Streisand called "laziness".

From the beginning, she was determined that nothing would stop her acquiring the status of superstar, and that meant conquering Hollywood. Barbara Joan Streisand, from Williamsburg, Brooklyn was going to be special. On her first album, she had sung a Schmidt and Jones song called *Much More*. In it, there was a line that must have come straight from the heart: "Please, God, please don't let me be normal..." Hollywood proved that she wasn't.

Streisand as Fanny Brice opens her coat to reveal a yellow nightgown in a still from Columbia Pictures *Funny Girl*. "Streisand single-handedly changed the Hollywood standard of beauty. And thereby did nothing less than change how America defined beauty" – Tom Santopietro, *The Importance of Being Barbra*.

funny girl, happy girl

Planning the film version of *Funny Girl* turned out to be a wild game of musical chairs. Streisand was not first choice for the role of Fanny Brice. The original director (Jerome Robbins) approached Mary Martin for the part, and then offered it to Anne Bancroft. She didn't like the songs, so Robbins considered Eydie Gorme or Carol Burnett before becoming disgruntled himself and leaving the project. Bob Fosse became the next director and it was he who brought Streisand on board.

Fosse then resigned. Sidney Lumet wasn't interested. The next director, Garson Kanin, lasted a very short while before being replaced by William Wyler, who saw the film through to completion. The surprise choice for the part of Fanny's husband Nick Arnstein was Omar Sharif. It seemed an unlikely pairing. Sharif had not been an admirer of Streisand. Rumor had it that he said: "I think her biggest problem is that she wants to be a woman and she wants to be beautiful..."

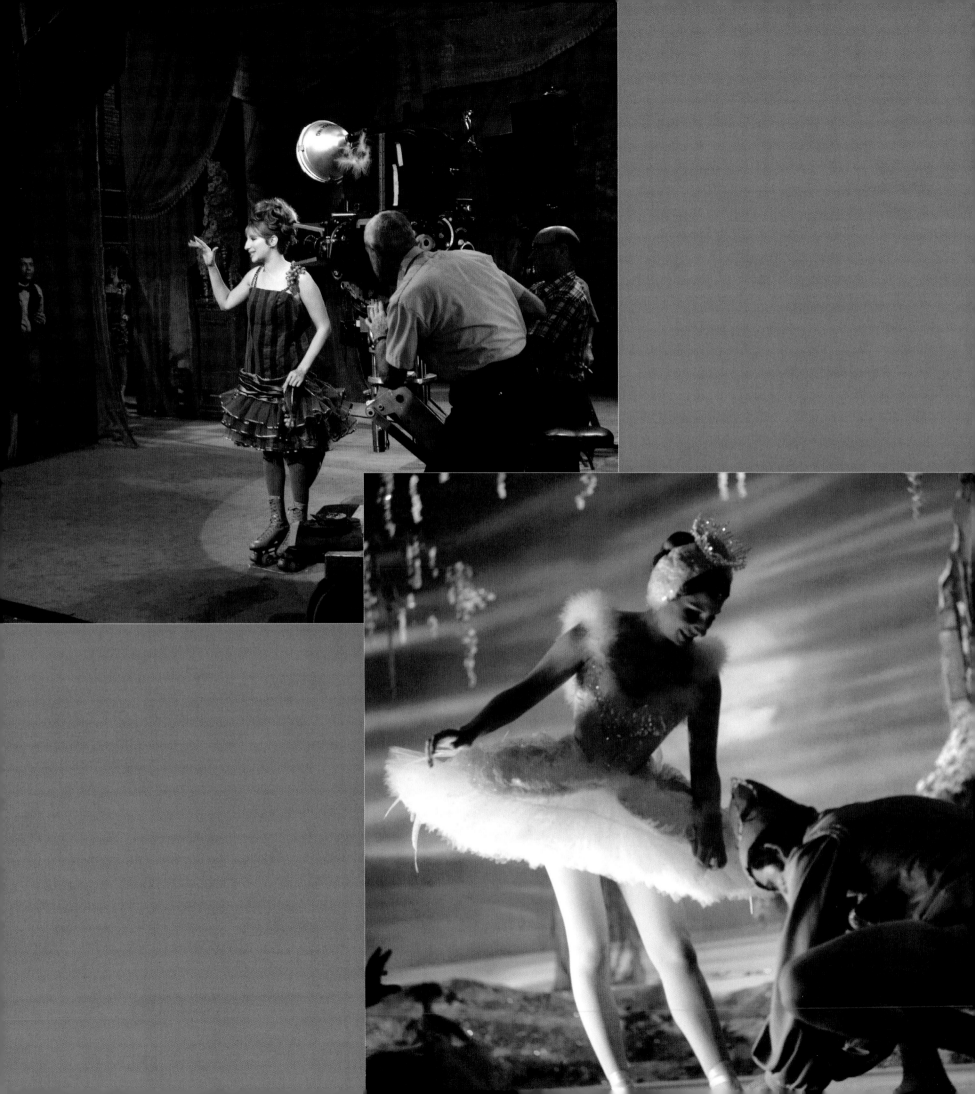

Left to right: Four shots from the set of *Funny Girl* – Streisand about to step off on the roller-skating sequence; Streisand as *prima ballerina*; Streisand as the on-stage bride in the *Ziegfeld Follies*; Omar Sharif as Nick Arnstein woos Streisand as Fanny Brice.

Stills and on-set pictures from *Funny Girl*.

Far left, top: Director William Wyler prepares his star for a shot. At first Wyler declined the invitation to direct a musical, as he was deaf in one ear. But he enjoyed the experience of working with Streisand to such an extent that other players in the film criticised him for always putting Streisand first.

Far left, below: Streisand and Omar Sharif share an intimate moment.

Omar Sharif changed his mind about Streisand once the pair met and started working together. Sharif fell for his co-star – a rare happening for a man who was usually more interested in playing cards than dating women. In the film, Sharif sang the number *You Are a Woman, I Am a Man* to Streisand. Whether, as the song says "she claimed him... and tamed him" is not known, but the romance was badly timed, for it took place during the Arab-Israeli Six Day War. This created difficulties for Sharif.

His films were banned in some Arab countries because he had made love on screen to a Jewish woman. In a later interview, Sharif said: "There were a lot of people asking 'What do you think of these press reports saying you kissed Barbra Streisand?' I said, 'Neither in my professional nor in my private life do I ask a girl her nationality or her religion before I kiss her. That has nothing to do with it.'" The problem for Streisand was nearer home. Her husband, Elliott Gould began to complain about her "dates" with Sharif.

The film was a tremendous critical and financial success, grossing $50.5 million at the box office. Streisand was nominated for an Academy Award as Best Actress in a Leading Role. Competition was fierce that year and eventually Streisand shared the Oscar with Katharine Hepburn (*The Lion in Winter*). Streisand had become a movie star, and played the part to perfection, living in a gated mansion, refusing to give interviews, and turning down all requests to give live concerts.

Left: Streisand is presented to Princess
Margaret (or maybe it was the other way
round) at the European premiere of *Funny
Girl*, January 16, 1969.
Above: Streisand and Omar Sharif (on
right) at the French premiere of *Funny Girl*.
Following pages left: Streisand poses in
front of rave reviews for *Funny Girl*.
Following pages right: Streisand in front
of poster of *Funny Girl* outside the famous
Broadway cinema, The New Amsterdam
Theater.

"Barbra's performance in 'Funny Girl' is the most accomplished, original, enjoyable musical co... performance ever pu... on film!"

— Joseph Morgenstern, Newsweek Maga...

"The musical blo... movie season, ... has arrived a...

— Judith Crist — NB...

'When Barb... it is one o...

When 20th Century Fox decided to make a film of the musical *Hello, Dolly!* the stage show had been running on Broadway for three years, with Carol Channing in the title role of Dolly Levi. Channing was not pleased when she heard that Streisand was to play the lead in the film version. "I was suicidal. I felt like jumping out of a window. I felt like someone had kidnapped my part."

Later, however, Channing was generous later in her appraisal of Streisand's performance in the movie ("Barbra has a tremendous creative force – she is so good..."). Streisand herself had some reservations: "I did feel that Dolly was a story of older people and that they should hire Elizabeth Taylor to play her... But when everybody seemed to be against me as Dolly... I took up the challenge." It was a typical example of Streisand's spirit.

Two publicity shots for the film *Hello, Dolly!*
The studio took elaborate care over
Streisand's costumes, hats and accessories,
filming a series of tests on April 12 and 19,
1968. The time and expense was worth it; the
film and Irene Sharaff won an Academy Award
nomination for Best Costume Design.

Left: A still from *Hello, Dolly!* which does a lot to support Streisand's claim than she was too attractive to play the part of Fanny Brice.

Above: Director Gene Kelly leads Streisand through her steps for one of the dance routines in the film. The film should have sparkled, but there were disagreements between Kelly and the choreographer Michael Kidd.

It had all started so well. When Gould and Streisand first dated, they had fun (*far left*). There are stories of snowball fights and of them both merrily throwing food at each other in restaurants. By the late 1960s the fun was largely over, and strain was beginning to show for Gould (*left*) and for Streisand (*below*).

Not all of Streisand's outfits were flattering. This *Art Nouveau*, 1930s Air Ace, neo-Cubist ski-outfit may have seemed a good idea at the time (1969), but it has not weathered well. Nonetheless, it does seem to have stopped everyone in their tracks when Streisand entered a room, which was probably the effect she was seeking.

Opposite: Stars gather at the 26th Annual Golden Globe Awards ceremony at the Cocoanut Grove nightclub, Ambassadors Hotel, Los Angeles, February 24, 1969: (*left to right*) Barbara Bain, Gregory Peck (Golden Globe Cecil B. De Mille Award), Streisand (for *Hello, Dolly!*), Martin Landau.
Left: Another opening, another gown… The cameras click as Streisand arrives at yet another Hollywood premiere.

Hello Dolly! received mixed reviews, but on the whole it was probably a better movie than Streisand herself thought it was. Though she claimed to share Dolly's fun in "bargaining" and to understand Dolly's experience as "a woman who had loved and lost", she seemed to have had problems in identifying herself with the character she was playing. "I have very little in common with a character like Dolly, who fixes other people up and lives other people's lives."

"I really didn't respond to the Broadway show," Streisand wrote, calling it "a piece of fluff". Dolly was not her kind of woman;

Streisand would have preferred the role of Medea. "Dolly takes place in an age before people realized they hated their mothers – the whole Freudian thing. So it wasn't something I could delve psychologically into too deeply, but I could have fun with Dolly and get days off because I didn't have to be in every single scene for once."

She called it her "last big voice picture". It was a mistake, but not a serious one personally, for the film only came to life when she was on screen. And, despite her reservations, Streisand was nominated for a Golden Globe Award as Best Motion Picture Actress – Musical or Comedy.

chapter 2

the seventies

No true superstar can allow herself to be fazed when she looks back at her own success. In the first decade of her professional life Streisand had released thirteen albums; starred in a Broadway musical; won nine awards (four Grammys, two Emmys, one Tony, one Oscar, and the ASCAP Pied Piper Award); and achieved legendary status. Lesser beings might be shaken by such a CV, superstars find challenge in it. In the 1960s, Streisand had excelled as a performer. In the 1970s, she was to show that she could also write, produce, and direct.

"...Mirror, Mirror, on the wall... who is the fairest of them all?..." By 1969 Streisand had made her point. The nose was not a problem, but an emblem. And even her worst enemies would have had to admit that she was far more beautiful than Durante.

the political arena

Early in 1970, Streisand gave an interview to *Time* magazine, in which she described changes that had taken place in her personality. "Being very to the point and blunt used to be a weapon for me. But I'm not as defensive anymore. I just really am blunt. That saves me a lot of time and also loses a lot of friends." She had never lacked belief in herself, but she was now determined to put that belief to the test.

She entered the field of politics. Nixon was in the White House and the Vietnam War was at its height. It was the time of early Gay Pride marches, of the Kent State shootings, of Black Power. There was much for committed liberals to do. Streisand campaigned from a flatbed truck for "Battling" Bella Abzug, the Democrat for New York in the House of Representatives, a move that has been described as 'one loudmouthed Jewish broad supporting another.'

The campaign was successful, but it was also a brave move that could have lost Streisand even more friends. Two years later, she was actively involved in the presidential election when she gave public support to the Democrat candidate, George McGovern. Her 1972 album *Live Concert at the Forum* was released to provide funds for the campaign. She was making sure that her name featured prominently on Nixon's list of enemies.

Barbra Streisand poses for the camera with
sandwich on a Chicago street, 1970. In a
later interview she said:
"I still like to eat hot dogs. The only
difference is that now, instead of eating them
inside the delicatessen, I munch them in the
back seat of our Bentley parked outside..."

career moves

Despite her new found confidence,
Streisand's professional career threatened
to take some strange turns in the early
1970s. She regretted her decision to be
photographed nude for *High Society*
magazine, and later had the pictures
removed. She flirted for a while with the
idea of making a rock album, before being
reluctantly persuaded by record producer
Richard Perry to go for an album of
ballads instead. Thirty-five years later, Perry
recalled the all-night session that ended at
5.30 am.

"I was sitting at the piano with Barbra.
We're running through it, and she suddenly
says 'I can't do this, it's just not me.'" Perry
reassured her, telling her that, if she was
unhappy, he'd cancel the session, adding

"But I can't imagine that Barbra Streisand
would back down from a challenge. I
promise you this is going to be an amazing
experience and one of the most exciting
sessions of your career." It did the trick.
Streisand went into the studio.

What happened next staggered Perry, who
described how he got "goosebumps" when
Streisand sang the album's title song *Stoney
End* for the first time. "I immediately asked
her and everybody to come in and listen
back... While we were listening, she leaned
over and whispered in my ear, 'You were
right, and I was wrong, but it's nice to be
wrong...'" It was one of the greatest
moments in Perry's career. The song itself
became another Streisand hit.

Images from the 1969 Annual Academy
Awards at the Dorothy Chandler Pavilion,
Los Angeles, April 7, 1970.
Above: Streisand with Lisa Minnelli,
nominated as Best Actress for *The Sterile
Cuckoo.*
Right: Streisand with Jack Nicholson,
nominated as Best Actor in a Supporting
Role for *Easy Rider.*

Three portraits and two on-set images of Barbra Streisand in the early 1970s. Streisand wore the cap and vest outfit (*top, second from left*) in *What's Up Doc?* The portraits would seem to endorse her belief that she was too attractive for the role of Fanny Brice in *Funny Girl*.

a star is born

In 1976 Streisand produced and starred in the movie *A Star is Born*. It was made by First Artists, the movie production company that Streisand had formed with Paul Newman, Sidney Poitier, and Steve McQueen. Critics panned the film. Hollywood didn't care. Tom Santopietro quotes a pre-production prophecy made by an insider: "It would be nice if the picture was good, but the bottom line is to get her (Streisand) to the studio. Shoot her singing six numbers and we'll make 60 million." He was right. The film was a considerable commercial success.

It was not a happy time. Streisand herself did not get on with the film's director, Frank Pearson, and there was big trouble between Streisand's co-star, Kris Kristofferson and her boyfriend, Jon Peters, culminating in a verbally obscene altercation between the two near an open mike in front of an audience of 55,000 fans. The press loved it.

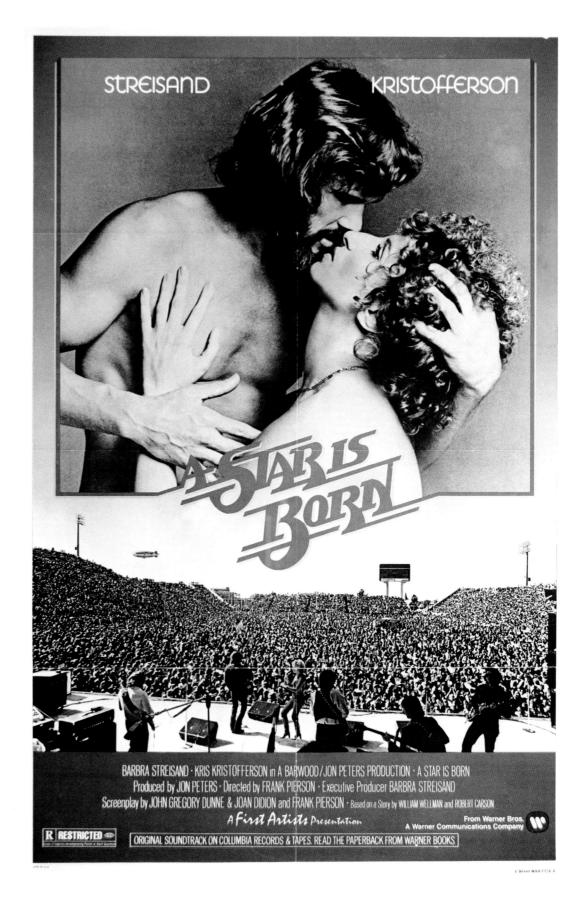

family life

Elliott Gould and Streisand met on Broadway in 1962 during rehearsals for *I Can Get It For You Wholesale*. Gould was the leading man; Streisand was the up-and-coming unknown. The following year they were married in Carson City. Their son Jason was born three years later, by which time the marriage was already in trouble as a result of his gambling and her extra-marital relationships (the list of supposed lovers includes Warren Beatty, Ryan O'Neal, Steve McQueen, Kris Kristofferson, Jon Voigt, Andre Agassi, Pierre Trudeau [the Canadian Prime Minister], Richard Gere, Omar Sharif, Richard Baskin, Liam Neeson, and – in ascending order of wild surmise – Bill Clinton, Dodi Fayed, and Prince Charles). Though not exhaustive, it is an impressive list. Streisand wasn't just acting feisty on the screen, she was feisty. She was a smart New Yorker, who could ad-lib real-life wisecracks as well as read them from a script.

Some commentators add to the personal difficulties that arose between Gould and Streisand, the professional problem that Gould's career never took off as fast and furiously as Streisand's did. He was said to resent being called "Mr Streisand". Interviewed by *Playboy* magazine in November 1970, Gould said: "I must admit that the happiest memories I have of Barbra are when we were living together before we were married." Seven months later he flew to Santo Domingo in the Dominican Republic and obtained a quickie divorce.

Opposite and above: Two pictures of Streisand with her young son, Jason Gould. In the picture opposite, Streisand and Jason are in a movie theater in 1971. Jason was five years old. It was a tough time for the family as Streisand and Elliott Gould were going through a divorce.

what's up doc?

After *Funny Girl* and *Hello, Dolly!* Streisand made her first film comedy – *The Owl and the Pussycat* in 1970. Gone were the glittering sets and the lavish costumes. Streisand was cast as Doris, a New York prostitute, and was clad in the famous flimsy nightie with groping hands on the bosom. At Streisand's request, the nude scenes were cut. Asked by a columnist if she would be singing in the film, Streisand replied "How many singing prostitutes do you know?" The critic Pauline Kael praised Streisand's performance, saying "she can wring more changes on a line than anyone since W. C. Fields".

Two years later came *What's Up Doc?*, directed by Peter Bogdanovich, with Ryan O'Neal as Streisand's leading man. Streisand played the part of a recidivist student and this time she did sing. There were two numbers – *As Time Goes By* (sung as a serenade to O'Neal) and Cole Porter's *You're the Top*. This was sung as a duet with O'Neal over the end credits and included a witty exchange about the famous Streisand nose. The film was a critical and commercial success and remains popular nearly forty years later.

Left: Streisand as the whacky student Judy Maxwell in *What's Up Doc?*
Above and right: On set with Ryan O'Neal. The film showed that Streisand had considerable comic talent and that O'Neal was a near perfect straight-man.

Above: Streisand and Bogdanovich at a
Gala Dinner.

Opposite: Director and star on the set of
What's Up, Doc? It was said that there was
a whole lot of kissing going on. At the
same time, Gould was having a less than
wonderful time making *The Special London
Bridge Special*, filmed in Arizona State Park.

the way we were

Arthur Laurents first met Streisand when he was directing *I Can Get It For You Wholesale*. He had been present at her audition, and had spent much time trying to tone down her runaway performance. He was also both the author of *The Way We Were* and the man who adapted the novel for the screen. It is hard to believe that he did not always have Streisand in mind for the part of political activist Katie Morosky in the 1973 movie.

Director Sydney Pollack enjoyed almost every minute he worked with Streisand: "It was like being given a great big present. Of course, when I went home every night and was about to sit down for dinner, the phone would ring. Guess who? So I not only got to direct her, I got to have dinner with her every night. I would go into work every day and I would watch her fill that role with so much longing and passion and poignancy and truth that it was a big high."

Morosky was a character tailor-made for Streisand – abrasive, committed, idealistic, and vulnerable. Her performance – opposite Robert Redford as Hubbell Gardner – gained her critical acclaim and both Golden Globe and Academy Award nominations for Best Actress. It was a smash hit at the box office, such a success that for years there were plans to make a sequel – Laurents did in fact write a full screenplay along those lines. *The Way We Were* is still regarded by many as the best film she has made.

Above: Streisand in rehearsal for her 1973 CBS television special *Barbra Streisand... and Other Musical Instruments*, August 8, 1973. Streisand was, as usual, relentless in her own application to the show, and had little time for those who sought to interrupt her.

Opposite: Streisand rehearses with Ray Charles, August 7, 1973. Charles performed three numbers – *Look What They've Done to My Song, Ma; Cryin' Time;* and *Sweet Inspiration.* The taping of this segment took thirteen hours.

... and other musical instruments

Streisand was required to make one more television special to meet the terms of her contract with CBS, who had waited for five years while Streisand concentrated on her film career. In November 1973 she fulfilled her commitment with *Barbra Streisand and Other Musical Instruments*. The show was directed by Dwight Hemion, who had worked with Streisand on *My Name is Barbra* and *Color Me Barbra*. The difference here was that it was made in London, and was breathtaking in its weird departure from the pattern established in all her other television specials.

It was poorly received by critics, though it scored respectable ratings – in the 1970s, it was almost unheard of for Streisand not to pull in a massive audience. The concept was possibly ahead of its time in that it sought to couple old and new songs (from Schubert *lieder* to *On a Clear Day You Can See Forever*), with an eclectic and eccentric choice of musical instruments and a comedy routine shared by Streisand and Dominic Savage, an eleven-year-old pianist. Some of it worked – the opening number was a triumph – but some of it didn't.

The critical nadir was a concert medley entitled *The World is a Concert*, in which Streisand sang to a variety of electrical appliances – kettle, sewing machine, vacuum cleaner, juicer. But the voice was in top form, giving a moving version of the Harold Arlen/Truman Capote little-known song *I Never Has Seen Snow*, and breaking the existing world record for the Longest Held Note (previously held by Ima Sumac) when Streisand finished the world tour with a twenty-seven second final note.

Streisand and Jon Peters, celebrity hairdresser to the stars. On their first date, Peters told Streisand never to keep him waiting again.

James Caan and Streisand in a still from the 1974 movie *Funny Lady*. Robert Blake was originally cast to play Billy Rose, and other names floated for the part included Hoffman, Pacino, De Niro, and Dreyfuss. Streisand was happy with Caan: "It comes down to who the audience wants me to kiss. Robert Blake, no. James Caan, yes".

funny lady

The Way We Were was a powerful, intelligent, and moving film. The following year Streisand made *For Pete's Sake*, an oddball comedy that was supposed to follow in the footsteps of *What's Up Doc?* and *The Owl and the Pussycat*, but dismally failed to do so. It was a puerile piece of clumsy slapstick, not worthy of Streisand's attention. And so, in 1975, she returned to the life of Fanny Brice, which had served her so well in *Funny Girl*.

Funny Lady was beautifully filmed (by James Wong Howe), the numbers were terrific, and the pairing of James Caan (as Billy Rose) with Streisand worked. Streisand convinced herself that the part had sufficient challenge to merit her attention, saying it was about "losing one's fantasies and illusions and getting in touch with reality". But critics thought the film all but destroyed the American musical and threatened to destroy Streisand herself.

For all its faults, however, *Funny Lady* was yet another in Streisand's relentless run of box office successes. The soundtrack album produced her eighteenth Gold Record; in fact most of the musical numbers sound much better than they look on screen. But Caan was good as Billy Rose, and Omar Sharif returned as Brice's ex-husband, Nick Arnstein, now in a minor role. *Funny Lady* was enough of a hit for cynics to voice fear that there might be a further sequel – Funny Granny.

Streisand was still in top voice and riding the ever-rolling wave of popularity. She was unquestionably a superstar, possibly the greatest in the world, and she lived her life in appropriately remote and well-guarded privacy. However, even superstars have to be seen in public occasionally, and in the mid-1970s Streisand was increasingly seen in the company of her new partner, Jon Peters, Hollywood hairdresser to the stars.

Her affair with Peters had a longer shelf life than was expected. An even bigger surprise to the media was the extent to which she allowed him to take control of aspects of her career. He co-produced her 1974 record *Butterfly*, an album that Streisand later identified as her least favorite of all, and was credited as producer of her 1976 Oscar winning movie and accompanying hit album – *A Star is Born* – both of which reached Number One.

Two pictures taken on the set of the Columbia/Rastar movie *Funny Girl*.
Opposite: Streisand and co-star Omar Sharif share a pastiche of intimacy.
Above: The two stars in more refined mode for a publicity shot. Some time later, Charlton Heston asked the director William Wyler if he had any problems with Streisand on *Funny Girl*. "Not really," said Wyler, "considering it's the first film she ever directed."

Streisand had some unhappy memories of filming *Funny Lady*. She later recalled: "When Ray Stark told me he wanted to make a sequel to *Funny Girl*, I told him, 'You'll have to drag me into court to do that picture.'" It might well have come to that, for Streisand's contract with Stark required that she make one more movie for him. Stark was a Machiavellian figure, the power behind the throne at Columbia and one of the old-school Hollywood tough-guy producers. Streisand eventually consented to make the film, perhaps because she saw it as her chance to emulate Liza Minnelli's Oscar-winning success with *Cabaret*.

After a decidedly bumpy ride, the film was completed in the summer of 1974. Streisand had made a wise choice. Most of the reviews were positive, the film earned $50 million, and was nominated for five Academy Awards – for Best Cinematography, Best Score, Best Song, Best Costume Design, and Best Sound. Moreover, she had fulfilled her obligation to Stark. She then sent him an antique mirror, on which she had written in red lipstick: "Paid in full". But there was also a note with the gift: "Even though I sometimes forget to say it, thank you, Ray. Love, Barbra."

Above: Streisand meets Queen Elizabeth II at the British premiere of *Funny Lady*, April 17, 1975. Also waiting in line are James Caan (on Streisand's left) and Lee Remick (*third from right*).
Right: Jon Peters and Streisand at the British premiere of *Funny Lady*, April 17, 1975. Queen Elizabeth is said to have personally selected the film for the Royal Film Performance.

Right: Streisand with fellow New Yorker David Begelman, head of Columbia Pictures, at the studio's 50th Anniversary Dinner. A few years later, Begelman was convicted of forgery. He had been cashing cheques made out to stars who never got the money.

Above: Jon Peters and Streisand at the 50th Anniversary Dinner.

Two images from a series of pictures that the photographer Terry O'Neill took of Streisand in her Beverly Hills home in 1976.

Right: Streisand surrounded by her haul of Awards up to that date – Emmys, Grammys, Golden Globes, and Oscars.

Left: A gleeful Streisand hugs her two Oscars. She won the first as Best Actress in *Funny Girl* 1968, and the second for Best Song – *Evergreen*, from the 1976 film *A Star is Born*. "Time won't change the meaning of our love..."

a star is born... again and again

In 1978 Streisand made her eleventh film, *The Main Event*. She was again paired with Ryan O'Neal, but this grimly zany comedy was no re-run of the wit and pace of *What's Up Doc?* The film gained some notoriety for having four scenes in which Streisand's bare backside appeared – perhaps because it had received official endorsement from Jon Peters as "a great ass". But the film was that very rare thing – a Streisand flop.

It didn't matter. Even her flop took over $60 million at the box office, and the album entitled *The Main Event* was yet another top seller. By now the Streisand phenomenon was achieving great sales with retrospective albums. Included on *Greatest Hits Volume 2* was a single that received three Grammy Nominations for *You Don't Bring Me Flowers* – a duet with Neil Diamond, with whom she had sung in the school choir at Erasmus Hall High School, back in 1959.

By the late 1970s, Streisand's trophy shelves were beginning to get a little crowded. The crazy Miss Yetta Marmelstein of *I Can Get It For You Wholesale* had become a highly respected actress and producer. And, save perhaps for Sinatra, there was not a singer in the world so famous, so talented, and so adored. As the 1980s approached, did anyone wonder "what do you get from a star who has already given everything?"

chapter
3 the eighties and nineties

On April 24, 1982 Barbra Streisand celebrated her fortieth birthday. For many women in showbiz, professional life ends rather than begins at forty, but Streisand has always been by nature an exception. Ahead lay more awards, more starring roles, more hit albums, and a whole new career behind the camera. Also ahead was an increasingly public commitment to politics and the causes in which she believed. Not for Streisand the timidity of other celebrities, who recoil from the notion of the politically engaged star. If the world wants to hear from Streisand, let them hear what she wants to tell them. (*above*) Streisand and Celine Dion celebrate following the recording of the duet *Tell Him* in November 1997.

Above: Streisand and friends: (*from left to right*) Diane von Furstenberg, fashion designer and publisher; Gloria Steinem, journalist and co-Convenor of the National Women's Political Caucus; Bella Abzug, former Senator; and Streisand, at a benefit for "Women USA" in Streisand's honour, December 1981.

In an interview she gave to Jack Newfield of *George* magazine in November 1996, Streisand spoke of events and conditions in her early life that shaped her social and political opinions. "We were really poor," she recalled. "I didn't have any toys or dolls... As a child, I felt like an outsider and an underdog in my own house... I was definitely a rebel. In *yeshiva* school they told us never to say the word "Christmas". But I wouldn't buy into that concept. I would say it anyway."

Streisand's first experience of seeing a Broadway play came on her fourteenth birthday, in 1956, when she was taken to see *The Diary of Anne Frank*, starring Susan Strasberg. Streisand was deeply moved by the play and claimed to identify "enormously" with Frank. Over the next few years, Streisand was to meet a number of women who reinforced her instinctive liberal, feminist views - among them Bella Abzug, Marilyn Bergman (co-writer of Streisand's hit song *The Way We Were*), and Shirley MacLaine.

"Most Hollywood liberals feel politics is impure," Streisand told Newfield. "They only want to help on a particular issue. But I wanted to actually elect the right people. That's the only way to change things." She will not run for office herself, however, saying: "I don't want to go around shaking hands and having babies pee on me." But, though campaigning has never come easy to her, Streisand has always affirmed her opinions. Throughout her career, she has raised her voice – in speech and song – for and against the causes she loved or hated.

Three portraits of Streisand in the 1980s. (*left to right*) In 1984, photographed by Dave Hogan; in 1983, the year of *Yentl*, photographed by David McGough; and in 1986.

yentl

In 1982 Streisand finally got round to making a film that she had been planning and working on since the late 1960s. It was Isaac Bashevis Singer's story of a Jewish girl in the 19th century. Yentl disguises herself as a boy, falls in love with a boy, but then marries a girl. Streisand's own passion for the project was engendered by two deeply felt emotions – a coming to terms with the loss of her own father, and a strong identification with the character of Yentl.

This was to be a project that would put all her talent and skills to the test. She was not only to star in the movie, but also to be its writer, producer, and director. If the movie was a success, it would be her triumph. If it failed, she alone would be to blame. Streisand was taking a considerable risk. She had been accused of megalomania back in the days of *A Star is Born*, but this was megalomania on a gigantically larger scale.

But *Yentl* was a huge success, on all levels. Commercially, it grossed over $63 million at the box office. Artistically, it won Streisand three Golden Globe Awards (for Best Director, Best Performance by an actress, and for Best Motion Picture – Musical/Comedy). The film also received five Academy Award nominations. For Streisand herself, it was also a professional triumph. Fans and critics alike realized it was no mean feat for a forty-one-year-old woman to play the part of a young boy.

Left: Paul Newman and Streisand at the 41st Annual Golden Globe Awards ceremony, Beverly Hilton Hotel, Beverly Hills, January 28, 1984. Newman received the Cecil B. DeMille Award.

Right: At the same ceremony, a delighted Streisand holds her awards for Best Motion Picture – Musical or Comedy and Best Director, both presented to her for *Yentl*.

Streisand with Richard Baskin at a post-Academy Awards party, March 24, 1986. As well as being an ice cream millionaire, at that time Baskin was also Streisand's musical producer.

putting her mouth where her money was

Earlier in her career, Streisand had raised her voice in song to support John F. Kennedy, Martin Luther King Jr., gays and liberals. But it was in the 1980s that Streisand revealed the real extent of her commitment to social and political causes. Her friend and songwriter Marilyn Bergman had recruited her into the Hollywood Women's Political Committee, and Streisand had an increasingly large circle of friends who were not afraid to show their true political colors.

Streisand was among the boldest of this Hollywood elite. The force within her came not only from the hardship of her childhood, but also from her Jewish faith. Streisand talked about her *tikkun olam*, her personal responsibility for repairing the world. "I was taught about charity, about putting money in a *pushke* for the needy. I was taught to invite a stranger to share your Sabbath dinner." On top of this, no matter how long she lived in California, she was forever a graduate of Brooklyn.

She remembered, too, times on the street when she was campaigning for Bella Azbug at the height of the Vietnam War. At the time, she had been scared, but she had felt what she called an instinctive attraction to Bella. "She was so smart, so eloquent, so opinionated... I didn't really enjoy campaigning or singing on a truck. I have always had this stage phobia. But I did it for Bella."

nuts

In 1987 Streisand was back in Hollywood
to make the powerful, and perhaps to her
disturbing, drama movie *Nuts*. The film was
directed by Martin Ritt, the screenplay was
Tom Topor's adaptation of his own stage
play, and Streisand co-produced and wrote
the music.

Nuts told the story of a high-class call-girl
named Claudia Draper, charged with
murder after killing a client in self-defence.
Streisand's character is determined to
prove that she is sane, and therefore fit to
stand trial, and in so doing is forced to
examine her own childhood, which
involved an abusive step-father and a
neglectful mother. Though by no means an
exact copy of Streisand's upbringing, there
were undeniable echoes from her past, and
Streisand wanted the film to display the
many ways in which women are exploited.

Richard Dreyfuss as defense attorney
Aaron Levinsky, and Streisand as Claudia
Draper in *Nuts*. Streisand and Martin Ritt
(the film's director) had an abrasive
relationship on set, and the final edit of the
movie was turned over to Streisand. This
may have been a mistake.

Nuts was a personal, rather than a critical or commercial success. Streisand may have had too much to say about the role and the abuse of women for the film's own good. The most powerful scenes are those in which her character (Claudia Draper) battles her parents, who are seeking to have her committed, and in which there are dramatic revelations about both Draper's psychiatrist and attorney.

Perhaps it all mattered too much for Streisand, who is at her most intense throughout the film. Critics felt it was too long, too strong, too loud. Streisand was perhaps a victim of her own success. She had proved again and again that she was so talented, so versatile, so professional. In the eyes of some, it was time she was brought down a peg or two. Such thoughts always come to critical consumers at just the wrong time in an artist's career, when so much has already been achieved and it is so hard to produce something new, something to cap all that has gone before.

Streisand was one of the principal financial backers of the film. Though it was considered a failure, the movie did make money. It wasn't enough. Streisand was disappointed by the lack of an Oscar nomination, but there was still plenty of determination to do better next time.

Above left: Barbra Streisand as Claudia
Draper in dramatic courtroom exchange
from the Warner Brothers movie *Nuts*.
Above right: Draper awaits her trial. Some
critics believed that Streisand's major appeal
to moviegoers in this role came from
remembrance of her past performances.

Three portraits of Streisand in 1990 by Terry O'Neill. He made his reputation as a photographer of showbiz greats during the 1960s, with pictures of Garland, The Beatles and The Rolling Stones.

The Fashion Connection... Streisand (*left*) with her close friend fashion designer Donna Karan, founder of the DKNY clothing label, at the 1991 International Antique Dealers' Show.

the streisand "look"

There has never been a time in her career when Streisand has not flaunted her sense of fashion. Compare the herringbone vest with Peter Pan-collared blouse that she wore for the cover picture of her first album in 1963, with what other female singers were wearing at the time. Put Streisand's picture alongside shots of Connie Francis, Doris Day or Brenda Lee, and it seems either the world has entered a new age, or she comes from a different world.

One year after that first album, on May 22, 1964 *Life* magazine ran an article on Streisand identifying the sudden nationwide frenzy to achieve the Streisand "look": "Hairdressers are being besieged with requests for Streisand wigs (Beatle, but kempt). Women's magazines are hastily assembling features on the Streisand fashion (threadbare). And it may only be a matter of time before surgeons begin getting requests for the Streisand nose (long, Semitic and... like Everest, "There").

And so it has continued ever since... often beautiful, sometimes ugly, always outrageous... the awful Arnold Scaasi pantsuit that she wore to collect her Oscar at the 1969 Academy Awards... the beautiful cape that she wore at the 1992 Council Designers of America Award Ceremony... the silken wings that she repeatedly spread during *A Happening in Central Park*... As in what she does, so in what she wears. The risk is always there, and 90% of the time, it's worth the taking.

Producer/director Streisand relaxes during the shooting of her 1991 movie *The Prince of Tides*. She received more praise for her work behind the camera on the film than for her performance in it, and welcomed finally being accepted as a serious film-maker.

the prince of tides I

After the critical and commercial relative lack of success of *Nuts* – no award nominations and a gross of only $34 million at the box office – Streisand decided once more to bring a variety of her talents to bear on her next Hollywood project, a film of Pat Conroy's best-selling *The Prince of Tides*. For a strong story, Streisand assembled a strong cast – Melinda Dillon, Nick Nolte, and Kate Nelligan. Her own role was almost a reversal of that she had played in *Nuts*. There she had been playing a putative mental patient: in *The Prince of Tides* she was playing a New York psychiatrist.

As well as starring in the film, Streisand was to produce and direct. This combination of roles had worked well for Streisand in *Yentl*, not so well in *Nuts*. It was a film she had long been wanting to make. She saw it as a natural follow-up to *Yentl*, in that, where *Yentl* dealt with father-daughter relationships, at the heart of *The Prince of Tides* were those between mother and child.

the prince
of tides 2

The worry with *The Prince of Tides* was that Streisand was once again plunging into an analysis of episodes from her own past. On top of this, she had cast Jason Gould, her own son, in the role of the psychiatrist's son. There were accusations of nepotism, silenced when Gould turned in a sensitive and moving interpretation. Streisand's own performance came in for some criticism, ironically because – in the role of a psychiatrist – some of Streisand's old hang-ups seemed to re-emerge.

While Streisand was making the film, her own mother was stricken with heart problems that threatened to kill her. This threw Streisand's exploration of the relationship between mother and child into higher relief: "When I was faced with the potential loss of my mother, the movie became much easier... It took its place... That's what *The Prince of Tides* is about... learning to accept your mother." The closeness of the subject matter of the film, and the casting of her own son in the movie, led to its lively anticipation on the part of press and public.

By and large, the film's reception gave Streisand what she wanted. *The Prince of Tides* gained seven Academy Award nominations, including those for Best Picture, Best Actor (Nolte), and Best Supporting Actress (Nelligan). In addition, Streisand was nominated for the Directors Guild Award as Best Director, and the movie made $118 million at the box office.

Above: "Happy days are here again..." Streisand in lively mood in 1991, the year of *The Prince of Tides*.
Right: Streisand waves to fans as she attends the 64th Annual Academy Awards ceremony in Los Angeles, March 30, 1992.

Above: Streisand sings "... one love that is shared by two, I have found with you..." The song may have been dedicated to both Clintons, but maybe Bill and Hillary didn't share the same reaction.

Far right: In more sombre mood, Streisand sits next to Hillary Clinton at a United Jewish Federation event on April 8, 1995.

streisand the democrat

All her working life, Streisand let it be known that she was an active supporter of the Democrat Party. She had performed at Lyndon B. Johnson's inauguration gala in 1965. Back in the summer of 1970, she had campaigned for Bella Abzug. In 1986, she had staged her famous *One Voice* concert ($5,000 for a double ticket) in the grounds of her Ramirez Canyon ranch in Malibu to raise money for the Democrats to regain control of the Senate.

1992 was a busy political year for Streisand. She condemned the state of Colorado's anti-gay legislation. At the "Commitment to Life VI" gala, she savaged ex-President Reagan for his "genocidal denial" of the AIDS problem. And in the Presidential election campaign of that year, she placed her considerable political energy at the disposal of the Democrat candidate, Bill Clinton. How much she contributed to his success can never be known, but she was with him all the way.

Famously, she sang at his inauguration gala in Maryland in January 1993. The crowd rose to roar its approval as she made her triumphant entrance. She was there, she said, to fulfil the promise she had made to sing a certain song on this night. She looked Clinton in the eye and said: "This is for you and Mrs Clinton..." and softly began the Love Theme from *A Star is Born*. If there was a dry eye in the house, it didn't belong to the newly elected President.

Above and right: Streisand on the stump, taking part in a campaign to stop the impeachment of President Clinton, outside the Federal Building in Westwood, Los Angeles, December 16, 1998. "After spending more than $40 million investigating this President, they've come up with nothing to charge him with."

hands off the president

After twelve years of Republicans in the White House, Clinton's first Presidency was a huge success, and he was returned to power in 1996. But the second term was a troubled time. The Clinton administration was rocked by scandals, of which the most damaging was the Monica Lewinsky affair. When it became apparent that the President had lied to the people – to say nothing of his indulging in sex play during working hours – Clinton was in it, deep.

This was when Streisand showed that she was not merely a fair-weather friend.

When Clinton's reputation was in tatters and there were yells for his impeachment, she stood solidly beside him. During a Q&A America Online session, she drew a distinction between Clinton's dishonesty and that of his Republican predecessors in office: "...a lie about personal indiscretion is far less significant than a lie about illegal government operations, such as Bush with 'Iran-Gate' and... Reagan with Iran Contra... I support Bill Clinton because of the way he serves the country and cares for the well-being of its citizens..."

Asked whether she though Clinton had the moral leadership to lead the country, Streisand replied: "Our greatest presidents, Thomas Jefferson, FDR (Roosevelt), John Kennedy all were great moral leaders in the public realm, but all had questionable practices in their private lives..." She was unshakeable. "Our heroes – and especially Presidents, are not Gods or Saints, but flesh and blood humans..."

Right: Streisand at the Designs Award ceremony at the 1992 Council of Fashion Designers of America in New York City.
Above: Streisand with her longtime friend Donna Karan (*on left*) who won the Menswear Design Award.

Opposite: In happier days, Ken Joachim stands beside a portrait of his beloved Barbra Streisand in his *Hello Gorgeous!!* Museum, San Francisco, shortly after its opening, May 15, 1996.
Left: One of the Streisand mannequins in the Museum, photographed in June 1997.

the sincerest form of flattery

In May 1996, Ken Joachim, a former vintage clothing dealer, opened his store-cum-museum-cum shrine in the largely gay Castro area of San Francisco. It was called *Hello, Gorgeous!!* (Streisand's opening line in *Funny Girl*) and was dedicated to the diva that Joachim adored. Creating the museum had not been easy, but Joachim had taken inspiration from one of Streisand's most famous songs. "You know that song she sings," he told the *New York Times,* "Don't Rain on My Parade? That's the attitude I took about this, and it took on a life of its own." It was a brave venture. Joachim had

mortgaged his own home to raise funds to create the museum.

At first, sufficient fans and devotees of Streisand paid their $2 to visit the Museum. They came to see the dozens of portraits of Streisand and, in some cases, to take advantage of the special services that Joachim offered, which included a makeover that turned them into replicas of their heroine, including the Streisand nose ($79 extra) and a 1960s Streisand style wig ($125 extra). But it was not long before *Hello Gorgeous!!* failed to dazzle. The

crowds dwindled. It *did* rain on Joachim's parade, and in 1998 the Museum closed for good.

Joachim was reported as saying: "It (is) difficult for me to respectfully own and operate a dedicated public monument to someone I have learned is not very truthful or nice." Fans were outraged.

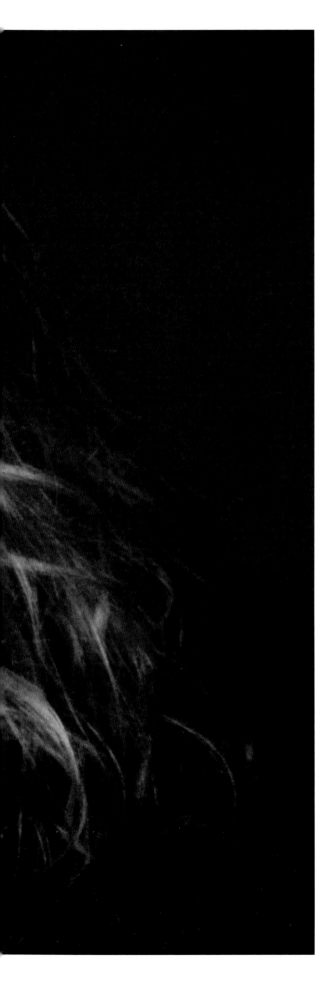

Life imitates Art (*see pages 128–129*).
Streisand in pensive mood replicates her
portrayal of Claudia Draper in *Nuts*.

Another ceremony, another stunning outfit... Streisand gives the *paparazzi* what they long for, a star cock-a-hoop with happiness, in Miranda Shen's photograph from the 1990s.

enter prince charming

Streisand's marriage to Elliott Gould took place on Friday, September 13, 1963 in Carson City, Nevada. It was a secret wedding, no fuss, no press, no fans. The marriage produced one child, Jason Gould, and ended in 1971. "I was very young, she was very young," said Gould, "and we went as far as we could together." Though there were subsequently many men in Streisand's life, most of them either were not available as spouses or did not appeal sufficiently to Streisand in that role. Twenty-seven years were to pass before she married again.

In 1996 a new Prince Charming entered Streisand's life. He was Hollywood actor James Brolin, whose account of their first meeting suggests it was an insult that first drew them together: "It was almost like a blind date. I had just cut off all my dyed hair and she came up to me and said 'who screwed up your hair', and I went 'Boy, somebody in this room is telling the truth.

This is great'." Two years to the day after that first meeting, in the wake of a very carefully prepared pre-nuptial agreement, Streisand and Brolin were married in Streisand's Malibu ranch.

Appropriately, for it cost $1 million, it was not a simple ceremony. Wearing a low-cut, crystal encrusted wedding gown with a fifteen-foot veil, designed by her friend Donna Karan, Streisand and Jason Gould descended a flight of stairs, to the strains of *The Wedding March* and *The Four Horsemen of the Apocalypse, and entered* a living room festooned with lilies-of-the-valley, gardenias, and 4,000 roses. There were bridesmaids, a ring bearer, a flower girl – all in pink – and the reception was held in a 2,800 square foot marquee by the swimming pool, which was laced with pink water lilies and floating candles. The evening ended with Streisand singing two love songs to her new husband.

living happily ever after

Following a honeymoon in the Channel Islands near Santa Barbara, Streisand got to work on a new album of love songs. *A Love Like Ours* was planned and designed as Streisand's tribute to Brolin, with an accompanying booklet of photographs of the wedding itself, and of the happy couple strolling on the beach, bathed in the light of a setting sun. The songs were of mixed quality, but all were explicitly romantic. "When love like ours arrives, we guard it with our lives," sang Streisand, but for once her usually impeccable taste deserted her. One of Streisand's best biographers

slapped the label "greetings card mush" on the entire exercise.

At least by Hollywood standards, however, the marriage itself is a considerable success. Streisand reportedly told Dustin Hoffman (her co-star on *Meet the Fockers*) that she and Brolin enjoyed sex six times a week and still found time for painting and gardening together. When asked "who wears the pants in the marriage," Brolin happily replied "she does".

Unsurprisingly, marriage in no way slowed down Streisand's creative flow. She continued to produce and direct, and continued to rake in the awards. In 2000 there was the Golden Globe Cecil B. DeMille Lifetime Achievement Award, and in 2001 the American Film Institute Achievement Award. And the albums – new or compilations – went on selling and selling...

Left to right: A few months before their wedding, Brolin and Streisand arrive at the White House for a state dinner in honor of Tony and Cherie Blair, February 5, 1998; Brolin and Streisand at the 69th Annual Academy Awards in Los Angeles, March 24, 1997; Streisand and Brolin at the Hollywood Walk of Fame ceremony for Brolin, August 27, 1998, eight weeks after the wedding.

chapter
4 barbra now

On April 24, 2007, Barbra Streisand celebrated her 65th birthday. She remained, in her own words, "a feminist, Jewish, opinionated, liberal woman". She still pushed a lot of buttons. She had come out of semi-retirement to raise money for and the awareness of those causes she so passionately believed in – political, social, environmental. She was good at raising money. Tickets for her concerts were always in hot demand. Every new album she released struck gold. And, as a good business woman, she was happy to auction clothes (*above*), jewellery (*right*) and memorabilia if the end justified the means.

Above: Streisand receives the National Medal of Arts Award from President Clinton, Washington DC, December 20, 2000.

Far right: Together again... ex-President Clinton and Streisand at the 2nd Annual Global Initiative Meeting, New York City, September 22, 2006.

I commit to make a difference in the fight against climate change

a national institution

Streisand entered the new millennium as one of the richest, most famous, most loved, and most respected entertainers of all time. Her contribution to the joy and gladness of her fellow citizens of the United States was marked by a special award. On 20 December 2000, in Washington DC's DAR Constitution Hall, Streisand was presented with the National Medal of Arts Award by her friend and President, Bill Clinton. It was perhaps the greatest of all possible tributes to Streisand the artiste.

Though there may have been personal reasons why Clinton was especially happy to present this one award, he delivered the citation in his customary dry, flat-toned voice. Nevertheless, the words he spoke were fair and fitting to a woman who had become a national showbiz institution: "Few performing artists are instantly recognized by only their first name, but when you mention Barbra, the whole world knows her voice, her face, her capacity to touch the deepest chords in our being... Barbra Streisand has been without peer, whether on stage, screen, or

in the director's chair... She has been a singular presence... She has a great mind, an enormous creative capacity, a huge heart, and the voice of a generation. I'm glad we have this honor to give her, and I thank her for all she has given to us."

singing for her supper

Streisand attended the 53rd Annual Emmy Awards Show in New York for two reasons. The first was that she was there to pick up yet another Emmy. This one was the Award for Outstanding Individual Performance in a Variety or Music Program, given to her for *Timeless: Live from the MGM Grand*. This was her latest album, recorded live at the Las Vegas Hotel on the last night of the old millennium. There were forty songs on the album, by and large good-old-good-ones: *You'll Never Know, Something's Coming* (from *West Side Story*), *The Way We Were, A Sleepin' Bee* (from Streisand's first ever gig), *As Time Goes By...*

The setting for the ceremony was New York's Shubert Theater. The Brooklyn girl was back home, centre stage in the same theater that had witnessed her sensational debut in *I Can Get It For You Wholesale* almost forty years earlier. She had come a long way, but this wasn't to be the end of the road. The release of the *Timeless* album was scheduled to kick-start a new Streisand concert tour, and her old fears of live performances were still lurking within her. Perhaps significantly, she wound up the Emmy Awards ceremony at the Shubert Theater by singing *You'll Never Walk Alone*. Time would tell.

Above and right: Two moments from Streisand's performance of *You'll Never Walk Alone* at the Emmy Awards, November 4, 2001.
Left: Streisand receives a standing ovation, Shubert Theater, New York City, November 4, 2001.

Opposite: Streisand presents Robert Redford with his "honorary Oscar" during the 74th Academy Awards ceremony at the Kodak Theater, Hollywood, March 24, 2002. His citation read: "Robert Redford – Actor, Director, Producer, Creator of Sundance, inspiration to independent and innovative filmmakers everywhere."

Left: Sidney Poitier presents Streisand with the American Film Institute's Lifetime Achievement Award, backstage, before a gala tribute dinner to Streisand in Beverly Hills, February 22, 2001.

lifetime achievements

Streisand had spent forty years in California. She was one of the Hollywood elders, more than a star, one of that special "brother-and-sisterhood" of the all-time greats. Throughout her career, Streisand had chosen her roles, her co-stars, and her directors with care. She was always the true professional, but she was also always the liberal with strong views on such issues as civil rights, gay rights, and the position of women in society. It was never her ambition to become a politician. Nevertheless, she has always been that rare object – the politically engaged star,

and as such she was at the centre of a group of Tinseltown's finest who spoke out against injustice. Streisand vehemently declared: "Most Hollywood liberals feel politics is impure. They only want to help on a particular issue. But I wanted to actually elect the right people. That's the only way to change things..."

When she worked with like-minded others, important and lasting friendships were formed. Sidney Poitier was an old friend and business partner, with Streisand and Paul Newman one of the trio that

formed the First Artists Production Company in 1969. Robert Redford, her co-star in *The Way We Were*, had frequently worked with Streisand to raise funds for the Democrats. And in the early 2000s, the old friends were now meeting regularly on prestigious occasions. Lifetime Achievement awards were in the air.

Streisand attends the Governor's Ball that followed the 74th Annual Academy Awards at the Renaissance Hollywood Hotel, Hollywood, February 27, 2005.

the president and the showgirl

Nowhere else in the world do politics and showbiz overlap as they do in Hollywood. One week it's the Oscar selection, the next it's the Presidential election and, characteristically, Streisand has long played a leading part in both. From the time when she first met Bill Clinton at a small "meet-the-candidate" gathering for Democrats in 1992, she was sufficiently impressed to agree to perform at Clinton's inaugural reception - if all went well.

What sealed the bond was Streisand's meeting with the President's mother, Virginia Cassidy Clinton. Perhaps Virginia felt she had found the daughter she never had, and perhaps Streisand experienced mothering late in her own life. The relationship lasted only two years, for Virginia died of breast cancer in 1994. Streisand's immediate response was to endow a $250,000 cancer research programme in Virginia Clinton's name at the University of Arkansas Medical School.

Though the Star and the President had a special relationship, Streisand's admiration for Clinton was not blind. She disapproved of his 1996 Welfare Bill that shifted much of the responsibility for public assistance from the Federal government to the individual states. "I wish he had not signed it," she told one interviewer. "But I have great faith that he will change it. He's still a great president." Then she added, "Did you know that Hillary urged him to sign it?"

Opposite: Streisand attends one of the three days of sermons and pledges at the Clinton Global Initiative Meeting, New York City, September 20, 2006.
Above: A hug for and from the ex-President at the same meeting.

back on tour

In the forty years since *A Happening in New York* - her open-air concert in New York's Central Park back in 1967 – Streisand had given few concerts – the *One Voice* private party in the grounds of her own Malibu ranch back in 1986, a couple of dates at the MGM hotel in Las Vegas, and a brief tour in 1994. In 1967 she had forgotten her words. In 1986 she had experienced a moment of horror when the audience rose to their feet and Streisand could no longer see the teleprompter. It was time to exorcize any demons she may have felt were still lurking out there, time to give not just one concert, but a series of concerts, home and abroad.

After playing sixteen venues in the United States, she began her European tour in Berlin, at the open-air Waldbuehne Arena where 17,000 fans gave her a rapturous welcome. She gave them a taste of *The Way We Were* and then thanked them for their welcome, said how happy she was to be in the land of Beethoven, Bach and Brahms (hinting at a fourth great "B" composer), and quoted a line which she attributed to Goethe: "At the moment of conviction, the entire universe conspires to assist you...", saying that it had helped her through her life.

Above and right: Streisand opens her six-week eight-city tour at the Waldbuehne Arena, Berlin, June 30, 2007. "I'm really glad to be in your city... it's filled with culture... and desserts..."

Left and right: Streisand at the O2 Arena, London, July 18, 2007. She followed the *Funny Girl* Broadway Overture with *Starting Here, Starting Now* and ended with *Don't Rain On My Parade.* The audience loved every minute.

Her Name Is Barbra
Property From The Career Of Barbra Streisand
To Benefit The Streisand Foundation

To order your copy of the
auction catalogue please visit
www.julienentertainment.com
www.barbrastreisand.com

Live and Online Auction
Saturday, June 5th at 11:00am
Exhibtion May 31st - June 4th
Astra West in the Pacific Design Center

JULIEN ENTERTAINMENT

LIFE

Opposite and left: Some of the items from the *Her Name is Barbra* Exhibition at the Takashimaya Store on Fifth Avenue, May 10, 2004. The sailor top is on the right of the middle row (*opposite*), next to the exhibition poster. The dress on the far left comes from *Belle of 14th Street*.

the streisand artifacts

On October 31, 2003 a year-long auction of Streisand's personal and professional memorabilia swung into operation. The object of the exercise was to raise money for The Streisand Foundation, a charitable organization that she had started in 1986. Over a period of twelve months "famous or cherished effects from the artist's life and wardrobe" were to be placed "on the block".

It began on eBay with the notorious see-through Arnold Scaasi pant-suit that Streisand had worn at the 1969 Academy Awards ceremony when she had won her first Oscar. In the spring of 2004 the accompanying, but far more upmarket *Her Name is Barbra* Exhibition and Auction opened on New York's Fifth Avenue, to be followed by an exhibition in London's Planet Hollywood, and another Exhibition and Auction at the Pacific Design Center in West Hollywood.

The pride of the collection were the costumes: by Cecil Beaton for *On a Clear Day You Can See Forever*, by Irene Sharaff for *Funny Girl,* and by Streisand herself (for an early nightclub engagement at the Basin Street East in 1963 and for her performance at the Washington Press Correspondents dinner of the same year when she met JFK. The top bid was $28,800 for the sailor top, designed by Streisand for her appearance on the *Judy Garland TV Special* in 1963.

once a democrat...

In the summer of 2004, Hollywood was split down the middle between those who supported George W. Bush, the Republican candidate and those who favored John Kerry, the Democrat. Streisand gave her support to Kerry, performing at a fundraiser concert in the Walt Disney Concert Hall, Los Angeles (introduced by Billy Crystal as "Woodstock for really, really rich people..."). A thousand couples paid up to $25,000 for a double ticket for a meal of *filet mignon* and shrimps, and a chance to hear Neil Diamond, Leonardo DiCaprio, Crystal, and Streisand. The event raised $5 million.

The highlight was a Streisand–Diamond duet, Alan and Marilyn Bergman's *You Don't Bring Me Flowers,* which Streisand and Diamond had not performed together for twenty-four years, in the days when Jimmy Carter had been in the White House, but Streisand saved her big political guns for a parody of her classic ballad *People.* To the partisan audience's delight she provided new lyrics: "Rumsfeld... We must get rid of Rumsfeld... He's the spookiest person in the world..."

Four years later, Streisand did all she could to obtain the Democrat presidential

nomination for Hillary Clinton. When Clinton lost out, Streisand switched her allegiance to Barack Obama, and sang once more for the Democrats. Tickets to a rare live concert at the Regent Beverly Wilshire Hotel on September 16, 2008 ($2,500 each) and the accompanying fund-raising dinner ($28,500 a head) together raised $9 million for Obama's campaign funds.

Opposite, above and below: Nicolas Sarkozy, President of the French Republic, pins on the Légion d'Honneur and plants a kiss on Streisand's cheek, the roses preventing a more face-to-face embrace.
Left: James Brolin and Streisand at the Elysée Palace in Paris for the Légion d'Honneur Award, June 28, 2007.

barbra today

On September 9, 1963, Streisand appeared as the warm-up for Liberace at Harrah's Lake Tahoe South Shore Room. She was introduced as 'the nation's newest singing sensation...' Twenty years later, Streisand listened critically to the first two albums she made. She was not impressed. "I just cringed... Although I had a purer reed-like sound in those days, I think my singing was often overly dramatic and screechy." More than a quarter of a century on, Streisand's voice is huskier and deeper yet retains all its old magic – in the words of Richard Rodgers, "with the depth of a fine cello or the lift of a climbing bird". At the age of sixty-four, her 2006 twenty-concert tour of the United States grossed $92,500,000, a world record.

As actress, singer, producer, director, composer, she has won just about every award it is possible for an artist to win. She has influenced the way society thinks about women, gays, poverty, justice, equality, and peace. She has kept faith with her fans and with herself. She has been an icon both at home and abroad, and a great ambassador for her country. When the French President Nicolas Sarkozy presented her with the medal of the Légion d'Honneur, he told Streisand "You are the America we love."

It has been a considerable achievement for the little girl from Brooklyn who was nicknamed "Crazy Barbra".

Barbra Streisand was created in conjunction with Getty Images. Particular thanks go to Jonathan Hyams and Paul Chesne at the Michael Ochs Collection. The design was initiated by Paul Welti but created and executed by Ros Holder. Author Nick Yapp worked with picture researcher Ali Khoja, Mark Fletcher edited, Liz Ihre was project co-ordinator and Mary Osborne led the production.

Fall River Press

122 Fifth Avenue

New York, NY 10011

ISBN 978-1-4351-1500-2

Printed in Singapore

10 9 8 7 6 5 4 3 2 1

All images courtesy of **Getty Images** including the following which have additional attributions:

t top, m middle, b bottom, all all

Agence France Presse: 142, 144, 152 (l), 153, 156, 158, 159 (r), 160, 161, 172, 173, 174 (all), 175; **Tim Boxer:** 74 **Dan Callister:** 143; **CBS:** 1, 16, 17, 18 (all), 19, 21, 24, 25, 26, 27, 28, 29, 46, 47, 48, 49, 100, 101, 102 (all), 103; **Columbia Tristar:** 56-7, 99; **Russel Einhorn:** 152 (r); **Fotos International:** 55, 76, 89, 90, 98, 122, 123, 136-7; **Murray Garrett:** 14; **Ernst Haas:** 69, 70, 71; **Brad Mankel:** 140; **Max B. Miller:** 73 (t) **National Archives:** 12, 13; **NOA/Roger Viollet:** 50; **Terry O'Neill:** 114, 117, 132, 133 (all); **Photoshot:** 94, 95 (all); **Roger Viollet:** 63; **Santi Visali, Inc:** 75; **Time and Life Pictures:** 8 (all), 9, 10, 20, 32, 40, 41 (all), 44, 45, 112, 113, 116, 118, 121 (all), 124, 134, 138, 139, 141, 145, 146, 147; **Warner Bros:** 84, 88, 126-7, 128-9, 130, 131; **Weegee (Arthur Fellig):** 6; **WireImage:** 159 (l).